OPPONENTS IN AMERICAN HISTORY

NATIVE AMERICANS AND EUROPEAN SETTLERS

DAVID LOUIS

PowerKiDS press
New York

Published in 2020 by The Rosen Publishing Group, Inc.
29 East 21st Street, New York, NY 10010

First Edition

Editor: Jane Katirgis
Book Design: Tanya Dellaccio

Photo Credits: Cover (left) Universal History Archive/Universal Images Group/Getty Images; cover (right), p. 5 MPI/Archive Photos/Getty Images; p. 7 (bottom) Fototeca Storica Nazionale/Hulton Archive/Getty Images; p. 9 PHAS/Universal Images Group/Getty Images; p. 11 Science & Society Picture Library/SSPL/Getty Images; p. 13 Print Collector/Hulton Archive/Getty Images; pp. 15 (top), 21 Kean Collection/Hulton Fine Art Collection/Getty Images; p. 15 (bottom) https://upload.wikimedia.org/wikipedia/commons/a/a6/Roanoke_map_1584.JPG; p. 17 https://upload.wikimedia.org/wikipedia/commons/6/6e/The_First_Thanksgiving_cph.3g04961.jpg; p. 19 (top) https://upload.wikimedia.org/wikipedia/commons/a/a2/JohnWinthropColorPortrait.jpg; p. 19 (bottom) Bettmann/Getty Images; p. 23 Historical Picture Archive/Corbis Historical/Getty Images; p. 25 (top) https://upload.wikimedia.org/wikipedia/commons/0/02/Vue_de_la_descente_a_Terre_Neuve_par_le_chevalier_de_Ternay_en_1762.jpg; p. 25 (bottom) https://upload.wikimedia.org/wikipedia/commons/c/c7/Washington_1772.jpg; p. 27 Stock Montage/Archive Photos/Getty Images; p. 28 https://upload.wikimedia.org/wikipedia/commons/d/d4/Trail_of_tears_map_NPS.jpg; p. 29 https://upload.wikimedia.org/wikipedia/commons/a/a4/Edgar_Samuel_Paxson_-_Custer%27s_Last_Stand.jpg; p. 30 Gabriel Olsen/Getty Images Entertainment/Getty Images.

Cataloging-in-Publication Data

Names: Louis, David.
Title: Native Americans and European settlers / David Louis.
Description: New York : PowerKids Press, 2019. | Series: Opponents in American history | Includes glossary and index.
Identifiers: ISBN 9781538345429 (pbk.) | ISBN 9781538343685 (library bound) | ISBN 9781538345436 (6 pack)
Subjects: LCSH: Indians of North America–First contact with Europeans–Juvenile literature. | Indians of North America–Colonization–Juvenile literature. | Indians of North America–History–Juvenile literature. | America–Discovery and exploration–European–Juvenile literature.
Classification: LCC E98.F39 L685 2019 | DDC 970.01-dc23

Manufactured in the United States of America

CPSIA Compliance Information: Batch #CSPK19. For Further Information contact Rosen Publishing, New York, New York at 1-800-237-9932

CONTENTS

A TROUBLED HISTORY

The history between Native Americans and European settlers has its fair share of treaties made and promises broken. It's a history of bloody conflicts, deadly disease, and destructive war. Some newcomers came to North America seeking religious freedom. Others came seeking fortune such as land and gold. The native peoples of the Americas were often caught in the middle, their own lands turned into battlegrounds by rival European empires.

As the newcomers spread across the continents, many natives were forced from their ancestral lands. Throughout the changes, Native Americans tried to hold on to their homes, **culture**, and way of life. It's a struggle that has lasted centuries. Even today, more than 500 years after Europeans first arrived, tensions between descendants of the two groups remain.

RELATIONS BETWEEN NATIVE AMERICANS AND EUROPEAN SETTLERS WERE SOMETIMES PEACEFUL. AT OTHER TIMES, THE RELATIONS WERE MARKED BY VIOLENCE AND CONFLICT.

EARLY CONTACT

In 1492, European explorer Christopher Columbus landed on an island he called Hispaniola (today known as Haiti). He described the new lands as "rich and fertile for planting . . . and for building towns and villages." To the Europeans, the lands that Columbus discovered became known as the New World. They included North and South America. But the New World was hardly new. People had been living in these lands for thousands of years before Columbus arrived.

The stage was set for clashes between natives and newcomers. On one side, the European settlers came to the New World determined to expand their empires, gain new lands, and find wealth. On the other side, the Native Americans meant to keep their lands and homes.

NUMBERS OF NATIVES

Scholars still disagree on the actual number of people living in North America at the time Columbus landed in the Caribbean. Some put the estimate around 1 million natives, while others suggest about 12 million. Regardless, North America was home to dozens of native groups from coast to coast, each group with its own culture, religion, and politics.

HEAD TO HEAD

Today, historians often use the term "pre-Columbian" to describe the period of time prior to Columbus's arrival in the New World in 1492.

WORLDS **COLLIDED** WHEN COLUMBUS FIRST ARRIVED IN THE NEW WORLD IN 1492. AT THE TIME, THE AMERICAS WERE HOME TO A RICH VARIETY OF MANY DIFFERENT NATIVE AMERICAN CULTURES THAT FLOURISHED FOR HUNDREDS OF YEARS BEFORE EUROPEANS ARRIVED.

CHRISTOPHER COLUMBUS

MORE EUROPEANS ARRIVE

Many other Europeans landed in the New World during the late 1400s and the 1500s. This Age of Exploration was an **era** during which many European explorers traveled to far-off places around the globe. In the New World, John Cabot claimed some of the land that would become Canada for England. Juan Ponce de León of Spain explored the West Indies and what would become Florida. The Dutch, Swedish, and French also landed in North America and established settlements.

Relations between the newcomers and the natives were peaceful at first. But as more settlers arrived, they sought lands and riches for themselves and their countries back in Europe. Many of the Europeans also wanted to convert the natives to Christianity and described them as "**heathens**" or "beasts in human shape."

THE AGE OF EXPLORATION WOULD BRING PEOPLE FROM A NUMBER OF EUROPEAN EMPIRES TO THE NEW WORLD. THE INVADERS WANTED LAND, BUT MANY ALSO WANTED TO IMPOSE CHRISTIANITY ON THE NATIVES.

IN THE NAME OF GOD

During the Age of Exploration and the years that followed, many European nations wanted to spread Christianity around the world. Sometimes, settlers tried to convert their native neighbors through peaceful means. Many times, however, they used force. Some Europeans used religion as an excuse to take land away from natives. Many European settlers believed Christianity was superior to any Native American religion. Many of these settlers came to the New World to find religious freedom they didn't have in Europe.

RISING TENSIONS

Rising tensions between Native Americans and European settlers began not long after first contact. When Columbus returned to the New World in 1493, he found the settlement he'd left behind destroyed and the men who'd stayed there dead. Columbus and his army of 1,200 men turned on the native Taino people. They killed many people and captured hundreds of Taino men and women and enslaved them to work in mines and plantations on Hispaniola.

On mainland North America, things were changing, too. Spanish explorers known as **conquistadors** came with armies in search of gold and other riches. During the early 1500s, bloodthirsty conquistadors like Hernán Cortés and Hernando de Soto tore through South and Central America and the areas that would become the U.S. South.

MANY SPANISH CONQUISTADORS CAME TO THE NEW WORLD SEEKING GOLD AND OTHER RICHES FOR THE SPANISH EMPIRE.

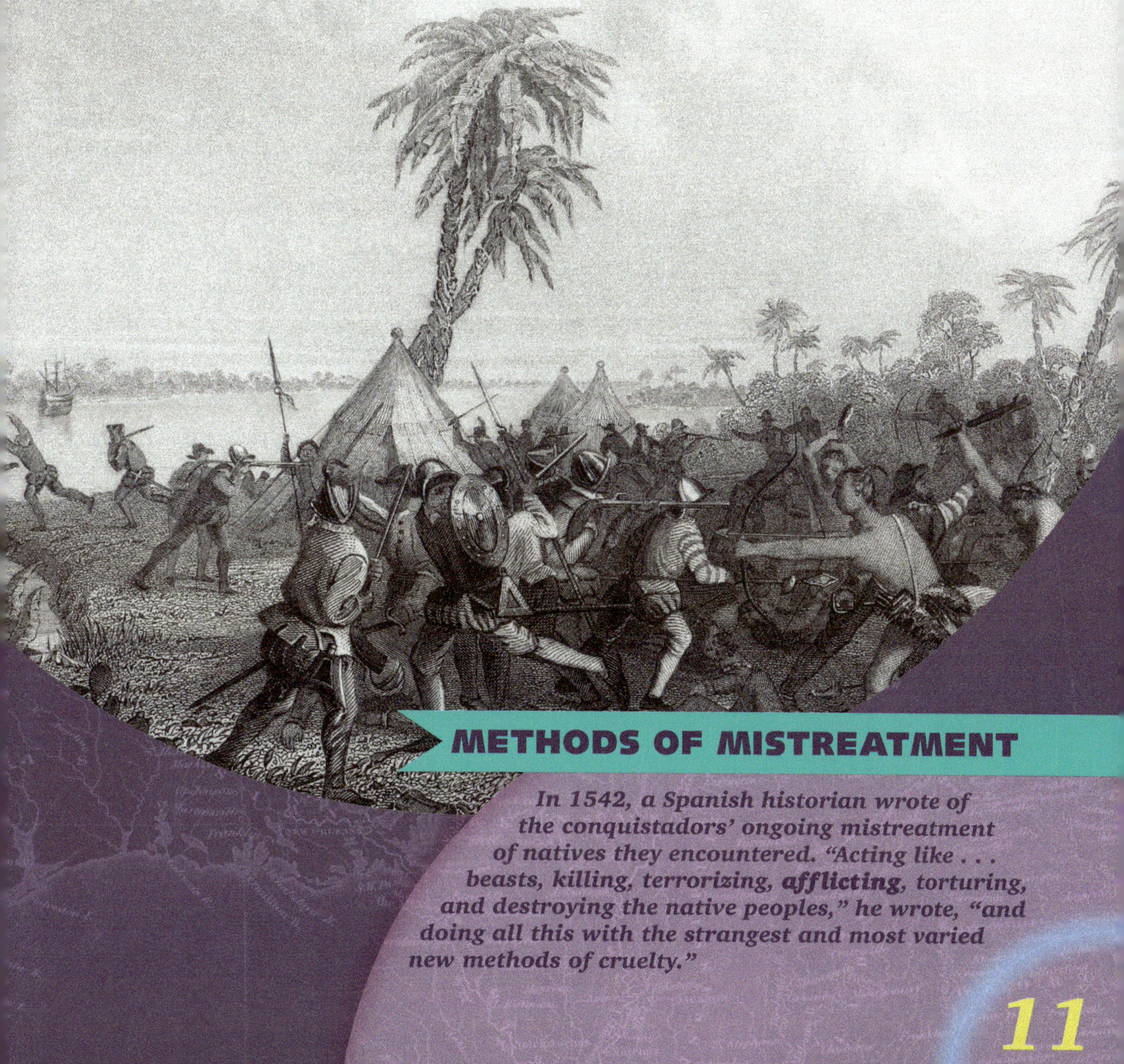

METHODS OF MISTREATMENT

In 1542, a Spanish historian wrote of the conquistadors' ongoing mistreatment of natives they encountered. "Acting like . . . beasts, killing, terrorizing, ***afflicting****, torturing, and destroying the native peoples," he wrote, "and doing all this with the strangest and most varied new methods of cruelty."*

DISEASE AND DECEPTION

Explorers such as de Soto were often the first Europeans the peoples of the native cultures of southeast North America met. In addition to modern weapons and powerful armies, the conquistadors also brought deadly diseases such as smallpox, measles, and mumps. Native Americans had never been exposed to these diseases, so they had no natural immunity. Smallpox alone may have killed as much as 90 percent of the natives who encountered these early Spanish explorers.

Stories of violence and disease brought by the Europeans traveled throughout the native nations of the New World. The spread of disease followed the explorers around North America, starting in the Southeast, then moving to the Northeast and eventually to the West Coast.

SMALLPOX

*Smallpox is a deadly and highly **contagious** disease. Before it was responsible for wiping out many native peoples in the New World, it killed many people in Europe and Asia. The spread of smallpox has been intertwined with the history of exploration around the world. In the sixth century, trade with China brought smallpox to the people of Japan. During the seventh and eighth centuries, travelers from the Middle East introduced the disease to North Africa.*

HEAD TO HEAD

Smallpox is one of the deadliest diseases mankind has ever known. In the 20th century alone, smallpox killed about 300 million people.

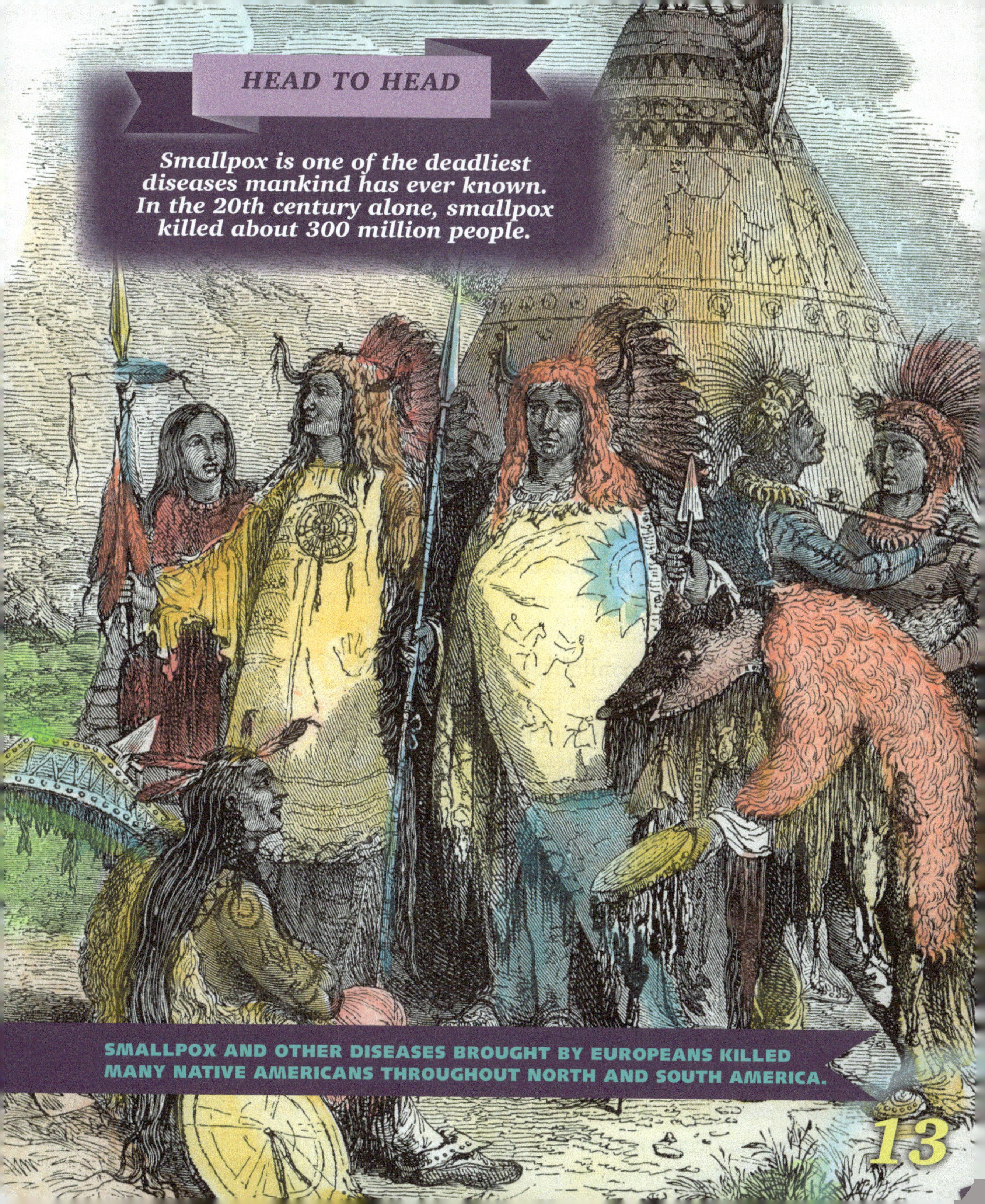

SMALLPOX AND OTHER DISEASES BROUGHT BY EUROPEANS KILLED MANY NATIVE AMERICANS THROUGHOUT NORTH AND SOUTH AMERICA.

JAMESTOWN

In the early 1600s, England founded its first lasting settlements in the New World. In 1607, settlers created the Jamestown colony in what would become Virginia. The local Native Americans had heard about the Europeans and the diseases they brought with them.

Life wasn't easy for the colonists. Food was scarce and bloody conflicts occasionally erupted between the natives and settlers. Tensions eased for a time when colonist John Rolfe married Pocahontas, the daughter of the Powhatan leader. An article published in 1609 reflects the warmer relationship between natives and newcomers: "They are generally very loving and gentle, and do entertain and relieve our people of great kindness."

As the years passed, however, the Jamestown colony expanded farther into Powhatan lands. In 1622, the Powhatans struck back at the Jamestown colony and killed more than 300 people.

WITH THE HELP OF NATIVE AMERICANS, THE JAMESTOWN COLONY MARKED ENGLAND'S FIRST SUCCESSFUL SETTLEMENT IN THE NEW WORLD. HOWEVER, THE PEACE BETWEEN NATIVES AND NEWCOMERS WAS SHORT-LIVED.

THE LOST COLONY OF ROANOKE

In 1585, more than 100 English colonists established a colony on Roanoke Island, off the coast of what's now North Carolina. When English sailors returned to the Roanoke colony in 1590, they found it deserted. There was no sign of struggle or conflict. The colony was just abandoned. No one knows for sure what happened on Roanoke Island. Some say local Native Americans killed the colonists. Others say the colonists ***integrated*** *with the natives. Today, the colony at the center of this lasting mystery is often referred to as "The Lost Colony of Roanoke."*

THE PILGRIMS OF PLYMOUTH

In 1620, another group of English arrivals landed on the shores of present-day Massachusetts. Some of these Pilgrims were Christians who came to the New World seeking religious freedoms they didn't have in England. They founded a new colony in Plymouth.

Conditions were harsh for the people of the Plymouth colony. Nearly half of the 102 Pilgrims died during their first winter in 1621. But things changed thanks to the help of the Wampanoags, the area's native people. Although the Wampanoags were suspicious of the Europeans, they knew the Pilgrims would be valuable **allies** against rival tribes. As a result, the Pilgrims and Wampanoags signed a peace treaty that would maintain good relations between the two groups. Peace between the Pilgrims and Wampanoags lasted for more than 50 years.

THE AGREEMENT BETWEEN THE PILGRIMS AND WAMPANOAGS USHERED IN A PERIOD OF PEACE.

THE FIRST THANKSGIVING

After the Pilgrims barely survived their first difficult winter, an English-speaking native known as Tisquantum or Squanto befriended the newcomers. He taught them how to plant corn and other crops. Squanto's knowledge helped save the Pilgrims from certain death during those first years at Plymouth. In the fall of 1621, the Pilgrims and Wampanoags celebrated the harvest and all the food it brought. This celebration of the fall harvest would later become known as Thanksgiving.

THE PURITANS

The next decades brought more and more English colonists, many of whom were Puritans seeking to create religious communities, to the shores of Massachusetts. Some of these newcomers founded the Massachusetts Bay Colony with settlements such as Boston and Watertown. By 1640, more than 40,000 Puritans lived in the colony.

The Puritan colonists followed rigid religious rules. These Christians **shunned** any other form of religion and had little respect for native cultures. The Puritans believed it was God's will for them to spread their settlements throughout the lands of the New World. In 1634, Puritan leader John Winthrop described the settlers' attitude: "For the natives, they are near all dead of the smallpox, so the Lord hath cleared our title to what we possess."

HEAD TO HEAD

First used in 1845, the term "manifest destiny" refers to a widely held belief that the United States should spread across North America and beyond. The settlers believed it was their mission to take the lands of the West—often at the expense of Native Americans.

JOHN WINTHROP

SOON, MORE EUROPEANS ARRIVED IN THE NEW WORLD SEEKING LAND AND RELIGIOUS FREEDOMS. SETTLEMENTS SUCH AS THE MASSACHUSETTS BAY COLONY RAPIDLY EXPANDED.

KING PHILIP'S WAR

During the mid-1600s, the English colonies continued to expand into places such as modern-day Rhode Island and Connecticut. The natives were increasingly upset with the newcomers. Many natives were angry the English were taking their land. Many felt English laws imposed on natives were unjust. Conflicts broke out between Europeans and Native Americans and threatened the peace.

These conflicts finally erupted into full-blown war in 1675. Metacomet, known to the English as King Philip, led the Wampanoags and other groups against the newcomers. As a result, the colonists declared war on the natives on September 9, 1675. King Philip's War was a long and bloody conflict. By the end of the war, more than 600 colonists and 3,000 natives were dead. Many more natives were captured and sold into slavery.

KING PHILIP'S WAR MARKED A BLOODY END TO PEACE BETWEEN NATIVES AND SETTLERS.

COLONIAL AMERICA

Following King Philip's War, relations between Native Americans and English settlers were never the same. The native tribes were crushed by the war. Furthermore, years of disease brought by the newcomers had destroyed native populations across the continent. The defeat was a crushing blow to the native tribes of New England.

Meanwhile, the Puritan colonists believed that victory in the war was a sign from God: it was time to expand the colonies. Following the war, the British greatly expanded their colonies in New England. The French also pushed farther into native lands in modern-day Canada and Louisiana. It was clear the flood of Europeans wasn't going to slow. Poor relations over the next decades forced native tribes to choose sides and forge **alliances** with the European colonists.

TRADE AND SLAVERY

The trade of goods such as fur, food, and weapons played a critical role in relations between natives and settlers. Tobacco was especially important as a well-paying cash crop in colonial America. In some places, such as Virginia, colonists pushed farther into native lands in a quest for more space to grow tobacco. To meet demands from Europe, the early tobacco industry relied on Indian slave labor. Later, when cotton became a booming cash crop, southern plantations would rely on African slaves.

FOLLOWING KING PHILIP'S WAR, COLONISTS MOVED INTO NATIVE LANDS TO FIND MORE SPACE TO GROW TOBACCO. THEY USED NATIVE AND, LATER, AFRICAN SLAVES ON THEIR FARMS.

CHOOSING SIDES

By the mid-1700s, many Native American groups became part of a power struggle between the French and the English. Many Native Americans chose sides when the French and Indian War exploded in 1754. The Hurons and other native nations sided with the French while the Iroquois Confederacy, a powerful alliance of six native nations—the Mohawks, Oneidas, Cayugas, Onondagas, Senecas, and Tuscaroras—aided the British.

The Revolutionary War soon put the colonists against the huge British military. Once again, Native Americans were divided. The war broke up the powerful Iroquois Confederacy as some nations sided with the British and others sided with the colonists. After their defeat in 1783, the British gave up their claim to many territories in North America. This unleashed a massive wave of expansion into Native American land.

AS EUROPEAN EMPIRES CLASHED FOR CONTROL OF NORTH AMERICA, SOME NATIVE AMERICANS CHOSE SIDES.

GEORGE WASHINGTON

A YOUNG PRESIDENT

One conflict that helped spark the French and Indian War occurred on May 28, 1754, when a British ***militia*** *attacked a group of French scouts, killing a French commander. A young and ambitious British soldier named George Washington led the attack. Years later, General Washington would lead the Continental army to victory over the British in the Revolutionary War.*

THE SPANISH MISSIONS

While other nations struggled for power in eastern North America, the Spanish claimed some western parts of the continent as part of New Spain. Spanish **missionaries** such as Father Eusebio Francisco Kino tried to convert native peoples such as the Pimas and Papago to Christianity. Kino also brought farming and irrigation practices to native peoples in what is now Arizona.

In 1769, Spain established its first permanent **mission** in California at San Diego. The Spanish missionaries also brought disease with them. In the mission system, many natives were treated poorly. Some were forced into slavery. "The resemblance to a slave colony is so perfect," French explorer Jean Francois de La Pérouse wrote, "that we saw men and women loaded with irons, others in the stocks; and . . . the noise of the strokes of a whip struck our ears."

THE SPANISH USED THE MISSION SYSTEM TO TRY TO CONVERT NATIVE AMERICANS TO CHRISTIANITY.

HEAD TO HEAD

Spain's mission system contained several buildings at each settlement. At the center of the pueblo (town) was the main mission building (church), which acted as the religious center. The presidio (fort) housed soldiers charged with protecting the mission and pueblo.

THE FRONTIER

After the Revolutionary War, the new nation looked to the West. As the frontier moved westward, more Native Americans met and clashed with settlers. The young United States government made dozens of treaties with Native American groups such as the Cherokees, Choctaws, and Creeks. The government said the natives would be allowed to live in peace in their own territories. However, these treaties were broken again and again.

In 1830, President Andrew Jackson signed the Indian Removal Act, a law which forced many Native Americans from their homes and onto **reservations** west of the Mississippi River. More treaties were made and more were broken. Conflicts such as Little Bighorn in 1876 and Wounded Knee in 1890 marked natives' attempts to retain their land and **heritage** in a new and changing nation.

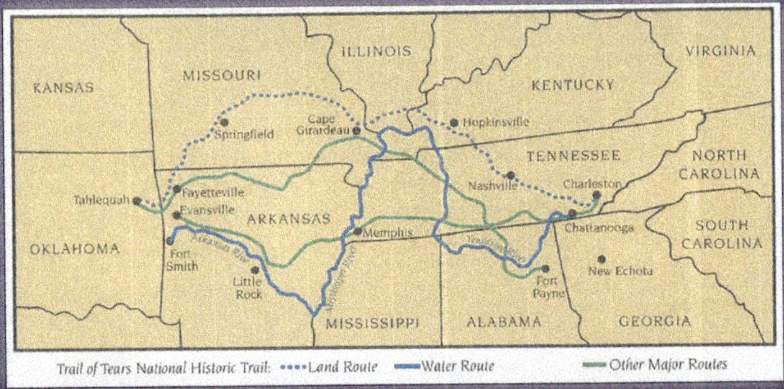

AS THE UNITED STATES EXPANDED, THERE WERE OFTEN BLOODY CLASHES BETWEEN SETTLERS AND NATIVE AMERICANS ON THE FRONTIER.

THE TRAIL OF TEARS

On December 6, 1830, President Jackson explained his reasoning for the Indian Removal Act, including, in part: "It will separate the Indians from immediate contact with settlements of whites; free them from the power of the States; enable them to pursue happiness in their own way." In reality, the law forced removal of about 100,000 Native Americans from their ancestral lands in the Southeast to reservations in the West. More than 15,000 people died during the move. These forced relocations are known as the Trail of Tears.

THE PRICE OF FREEDOM

Over the centuries, relations between Native Americans and European settlers have been full of broken promises and bloodshed. Even at first contact, European explorers enslaved Native Americans and took over their land. Later, settlers and pioneers seeking land and fortune continued to force natives from their homes.

Today, Native Americans still fight for their **sovereignty**. Their rights are often swept aside, many times in the quest for resources such as oil and natural gas. In a number of places, including Standing Rock Indian Reservation in North Dakota and South Dakota or the Arctic National Wildlife Refuge in Alaska, Native Americans still fight trespasses onto their lands. It's a story that has been repeated time and again over the centuries—and probably won't end anytime soon.

GLOSSARY

afflict: To cause pain or trouble.

alliance: A close association formed between people or groups of people to reach a common objective.

ally: An individual or nation working with others for a common cause.

collide: To bump into or smash together.

conquistador: A Spanish conqueror or adventurer.

contagious: Easily passed from person to person.

culture: The beliefs and ways of life of a certain group of people.

era: A period of time.

heathen: A term sometimes used to describe people who don't practice the user's religion.

heritage: The traditions and beliefs that are part of the history of a group or a nation.

integrate: To make a person or a group part of a larger group.

militia: A group of people who are not an official part of the armed forces of a country but are trained like soldiers.

mission: A community established by a church for the purpose of spreading its faith.

missionary: Someone who travels to a new place to spread their faith.

reservation: Land set aside by the government for specific Native American tribes to live on.

shun: To avoid, ignore, or reject.

sovereignty: Independence; the authority to govern oneself.

INDEX

WEBSITES

Due to the changing nature of Internet links, PowerKids Press has developed an online list of websites related to the subject of this book. This site is updated regularly. Please use this link to access the list: www.powerkidslinks.com/oiah/native